THE PARABLES OF JESUS

12 Studies for Individuals or Groups

GLADYS HUNT

the Parables of Jesus **BS**

Harold Shaw Publishers • Wheaton, Illinois

ISBN 0-87788-791-8

Cover photo © 1994 by Robert McKendrick

99 98 97 96 95

14 13 12 11 10 9 8 7 6

CONTENTS

INTRODUCTION

Jesus was a master teacher. His speeches weren't dull doctrine or abstract theology, but lively discourses full of illustrations, metaphors, and stories that caught and held the popular interest. Preparing this series of studies on stories told by Jesus—the parables—has renewed my wonder at his understanding of people and at how he communicated to their emotions and imagination as well as their intellect.

Have you noticed how often Jesus used the inductive method? Instead of telling his answers, he often asked questions to engage his listeners in the working out a solution in dialogue with him. He answered questions with more questions. He made people think.

The parables also provoke thought. In each one Jesus communicated truth about God or the kingdom of heaven that he wanted his listeners to remember, and so he told them a story. Who could forget how God loves lost people after hearing the stories of Luke 15 about the lost sheep, the lost coin, and the lost son? Each tale makes us ask, "Am I like that? Is God like that?"

Luci Shaw has observed: "[Jesus] takes the truth he wants to communicate, weaves it into a story rich in visual imagery, and suddenly those who are eager to understand can see new truth with the eye of imagination. When Jesus says in his stories: *this* is like *that* (God is like a landowner, his Word is like a seed) he makes reality clearer. He reminds his listeners of how important it is to have spiritual, or imaginative, 'eyes to see.'

"Robert Frost defined a parable as a story 'that means what it says, and something else besides.' And in the New Testament that *something besides* is the more important of the two. Jesus' stories have familiar settings. The farmer sowing seed, the employer hiring workers for his vineyard, the mustard seed, the traveler on the way to Jericho, the man who found a pearl—his listeners immediately saw a picture in their minds as Jesus spoke. He joined that picture to something besides, a spiritual reality he wanted them to see." (from "Seeing Metaphors of the Bible," *Christian Educator's Journal*, Feb.–March 1985, p. 26.)

A few of his stories needed explanation. Others, like the story of the Good Samaritan, have obvious meanings. Sometimes the disciples waited until they were alone with Jesus to ask for his explanation of a story. Some parables required persistent probing for the meaning. Only those committed to Jesus would follow through in trying to understand.

Most of the parables are found in Matthew and Luke. Only a few, those about the kingdom, are found in all three of the synoptic Gospels of Matthew, Mark, and Luke. For this studyguide I have selected the major parables and grouped them for maximum comparison and reinforcement in a discussion group.

The parables have spoken to me afresh, and I've been impressed again with the great truths they teach, for these stories give insights about God, his character, his kingdom, his people, and the rules by which the kingdom of heaven operates.

I am grateful for the loving support of the small group Bible study that meets in the Towsley home in Ann Arbor, Michigan, where I tested these studies before publication.

HOW TO USE THIS STUDYGUIDE

Fisherman studyguides are based on the inductive approach to Bible study. Inductive study is discovery study; we discover what the Bible says as we ask questions about its content and search for answers. This is quite different from the process in which a teacher *tells* a group *about* the Bible and what it means and what to do about it. In inductive study God speaks directly to each of us through his Word.

A group functions best when a leader keeps the discussion on target, but this leader is neither the teacher nor the "answer person." A leader's responsibility is to *ask*—not *tell*. The answers come from the text itself as group members examine, discuss, and think together about the passage.

There are four kinds of questions in each study. The first is an *approach question*. Used before the Bible passage is read, this question breaks the ice and helps you focus on the topic of the Bible study. It begins to reveal where thoughts and feelings need to be transformed by Scripture.

Some of the earlier questions in each study are *observation questions* designed to help you find out basic facts—who, what, where, when, and how.

When you know what the Bible says you need to ask, *What does it mean?* These *interpretation questions* help you to discover the writer's basic message.

Application questions ask, *What does it mean to me?* They challenge you to live out the Scripture's life-transforming message.

Fisherman studyguides provide spaces between questions for jotting down responses and related questions you would like to raise in the group. Each group member should have a copy of the studyguide and may take a turn in leading the group.

A group should use any accurate, modern translation of the Bible such as the *New International Version,* the *New American Standard Bible,* the *Revised Standard Version,* the *New Jerusalem Bible,* or the *Good News Bible.* (Other translations or paraphrases of the Bible may be referred to when additional help is needed.) Bible commentaries should not be brought to a Bible study because they tend to dampen discussion and keep people from thinking for themselves.

SUGGESTIONS FOR GROUP LEADERS

1. Read and study the Bible passage thoroughly beforehand, grasping its themes and applying its teachings for yourself. Pray that the Holy Spirit will "guide you into truth" so that your leadership will guide others.

2. If the studyguide's questions ever seem ambiguous or unnatural to you, rephrase them, feeling free to add others that seem necessary to bring out the meaning of a verse.

3. Begin (and end) the study promptly. Start by asking someone to pray for God's help. Remember, the Holy Spirit is the teacher, not you!

4. Ask for volunteers to read the passages out loud.

5. As you ask the studyguide's questions in sequence, encourage everyone to participate in the discussion. If some are silent, ask, "What do you think, Heather?" or, "Dan, what can you add to that answer?" or suggest, "Let's have an answer from someone who hasn't spoken up yet."

6. If a question comes up that you can't answer, don't be afraid to admit that you're baffled! Assign the topic as a research project for someone to report on next week.

7. Keep the discussion moving and focused. Though tangents will inevitably be introduced, you can bring the discussion back to the topic at hand. Learn to pace the discussion so that you finish a study each session you meet.

8. Don't be afraid of silences: some questions take time to answer and some people need time to gather courage to speak. If silence persists, rephrase your question, but resist the temptation to answer it yourself.

9. If someone comes up with an answer that is clearly illogical or unbiblical, ask him or her for further clarification: "What verse suggests that to you?"

10. Discourage Bible-hopping and overuse of cross-references. Learn all you can from *this* passage, along with a few important references suggested in the studyguide.

11. Some questions are marked with a ♦. This indicates that further information is available in the Leader's Notes at the back of the guide.

12. For further information on getting a new Bible study group started and keeping it functioning effectively, read Gladys Hunt's *You Can Start a Bible Study Group* and *Pilgrims in Progress: Growing through Groups* by Jim and Carol Plueddemann.

SUGGESTIONS FOR GROUP MEMBERS

1. Learn and apply the following ground rules for effective Bible study. (If new members join the group later, review these guidelines with the whole group.)

2. Remember that your goal is to learn all that you can *from the Bible passage being studied.* Let it speak for itself without using Bible commentaries or other Bible passages. There is more than enough in each assigned passage to keep your group productively occupied for one session. Sticking to the passage saves the group from insecurity and confusion.

3. Avoid the temptation to bring up those fascinating tangents that don't really grow out of the passage you are discussing. If the topic is of common interest, you can bring it up later in informal conversation following the study. Meanwhile, help each other stick to the subject!

4. Encourage each other to participate. People remember best what they discover and verbalize for themselves. Some people are naturally shyer than others, or they may be afraid of making a mistake. If your discussion is free and friendly and you show real interest in what other group members think and feel, they will be more likely to speak up. Remember, the more people involved in a discussion, the richer it will be.

5. Guard yourself from answering too many questions or talking too much. Give others a chance to express themselves. If you are one who participates easily, discipline yourself by counting to ten before you open your mouth!

6. Make personal, honest applications and commit yourself to letting God's Word change you.

THE SOWER AND THE SOILS

Luke 8:4-15

Jesus was at the height of his ministry. His reputation had spread and crowds were gathering everywhere he went, eager to hear what he had to say. His disciples perhaps felt a sense of euphoria in Jesus' great success; surely everyone would want to follow him. But Jesus reveals a realism in his evangelism by telling a story about a farmer who sows seed, some yielding a harvest and some yielding nothing. The story was simple, but for those who were really listening, it was packed with meaning.

1. From your own experience or what you have observed, what is difficult about growing healthy plants from seeds?

Read Luke 8:4-15.

2. Describe Jesus' audience for this story. What might they have felt and thought as they listened?

3. When the farmer went out to sow his seed, into what four kinds of soil did he spread it? How did the condition of the soil determine the farmer's yield?

♦ **4.** To whom did Jesus tell the meaning of the parable? Why did he speak in parables to the crowd?

5. According to Jesus, what does the soil represent? The seed? Why might he have been sad when he contemplated the possible fate of the Word of God sowed in individual lives?

6. Who are the ones along the path (verses 5, 12)? What lifestyle keeps the seed from germinating there? Name some "birds of the air" that the devil may use to remove the seed of the Word before it can take root.

7. What are the people like who represent the rocky soil (verses 6, 13)? What spoils the full growth of the Word of God in the life of a person on rocky ground?

♦ **8.** Describe those represented by thorny soil and what happens to God's seed in their lives (verses 7, 14). How might life's worries and pleasures weaken or crowd out the development of the Word in a person's life? Give an example from your own life.

9. What characterizes good soil (verses 8, 15)? How do those who are good soil receive the Word? What is involved in retaining and persevering in regard to the Word of God?

10. Compare Matthew 13:23 and Mark 4:20, observing the words that further describe the "good soil" of the heart. How do you explain the different yields of grain in these accounts?

11. In what sense do you have all four kinds of soil within you? How can you prepare the soil of your life for the most fruitful harvest, and really hear and retain God's Word?

12. What does this story tell us about Jesus' understanding of evangelism?

13. We are sowers of the seed of the Word of God when we share our faith with others. How does this parable help us to be realistic about the response to our witnessing? How should we sow?

THE TWO WEDDINGS

Matthew 22:1-14; 25:1-13

It's been said that those who know the value of time use it in preparation for eternity. How we spend our time reveals what is important to us, especially in the frantic pace of this decade's typical day. In these two stories Jesus reminds his hearers that refusing his invitation, or just not being ready, can have serious results.

1. One of my young friends, in distress over his family situation, said, "I wish the Lord Jesus would come tomorrow." When asked, "Why not today?" he answered, "I have a baseball game tonight." In what ways are you like this ten-year-old boy?

Read Matthew 22:1-14.

◆ **2.** Who gave the banquet and for what reason? Why didn't those invited respond to the summons? Why would people refuse to come to such a feast of joy?

3. Who did the king invite to the banquet after the first guests refused? What does this tell us about the king? Who do these people represent?

◆ **4.** What do verses 11-14 tell us about the qualification for attending the wedding feast? What might the wedding clothes represent? Why won't other clothes do, even if we think they look good enough?

5. From what we see in Matthew 21:45-46 and 22:15, what would this story have meant to the Jewish leaders?

6. Interpret the parable: What was the wedding feast, who was the king, and who were those who refused to come? Where do you see yourself in this story? What is your response to the banquet invitation?

Read Matthew 25:1-13.

7. The parable of the ten virgins was part of a larger teaching Jesus gave about future events. Skim Matthew 24:36-51 and summarize Jesus' teaching.

♦ **8.** Now look at the parable itself. Who were the virgins expecting? What uncertainty did they face?

9. While the bridegroom delayed his coming, what did the virgins do? What advantages did the the wise virgins have?

10. When did the foolish virgins begin to worry about oil for their lamps? How did they want to solve the problem?

11. What is the main point of this parable? What did the virgins' preparation (or lack of it) say about the level of their expectancy?

12. Are you satisfied with your own actions and attitudes toward Christ's return? What preparations must you make for the bridegroom's coming?

THE KINGDOM OF HEAVEN

Matthew 13:24-33, 36-40, 44-52

The disciples must have been puzzled. What kind of kingdom was Jesus talking about when he referred to the "kingdom of heaven"? They were a small group of not very impressive followers. What resources did *they* have to help him bring in this kingdom? The people who thronged to hear Jesus were unbelieving, but also curious. Would this kingdom of heaven solve any of their problems and do away with evil, especially the hated rule of Rome? Perhaps to quiet the anxiety of the disciples and inform his other hearers, Jesus told this series of kingdom parables—stories about hidden power and small beginnings.

1. If someone asked you what the kingdom of heaven is, how would you respond?

Read Matthew 13:24-30, 36-40.

2. In this first story Jesus told, what problem had to be solved?

♦ **3.** Why didn't the owner of the field pull the weeds in the field?

4. Who was responsible to weed the garden? When and how did the owner get rid of the weeds?

5. In Jesus' explanation of the story, who is the one that sowed the seed? Identify the field, the good seed, the weeds, the enemy, and the harvesters.

6. When are the weeds dealt with? Contrast the destinies of the good and the bad seed.

♦ **7.** With this parable in mind, why do you think God allows evil to exist in the world and does not get rid of it immediately? What makes the "weeds" so dangerous in the church?

Read Matthew 13:31-33.

8. What do the mustard seed and the yeast have in common? In comparing them with the kingdom of heaven, what was Jesus saying about the kingdom's power?

9. How would this truth have encouraged the disciples? How does it encourage you? Have you had an experience of this hidden power? Share it with the group.

Read Matthew 13:44-52.

10. How did each of the two men find his treasure? How did each one show confidence in its value? What would it mean to you to sell everything to purchase the kingdom of heaven?

11. What did Jesus teach about the kingdom of heaven in verses 47-52? About judgment? Compare this story with the parable of the wheat and tares.

12. In this chapter Jesus used seven similes for the kingdom of heaven. Review these stories and list the word pictures.

13. Which of these pictures best describes your own attitude or view of the kingdom? Why?

Pray together and ask God to help you recognize the kingdom of heaven in your circumstances.

THE RICH MAN AND LAZARUS

Luke 16:19-31

The increasing reports of people returning to life after being clinically dead have sparked speculative interest in life after death. In this story, Jesus pulls aside the curtain between this world and the next and gives us an authentic look at some of the realities of life after death.

1. What do you believe about life after death?

Read Luke 16:19-31.

♦ **2.** Give a description of the first character in the story, and what you imagine his lifestyle was like. Why is verse 19 such a tragic comment on the substance of a human life?

◆ **3.** Note the verb "was laid" in verse 20. What does this indicate? Contrast the lifestyles of Lazarus and the rich man.

4. What common event happened to both men? How do you think their funerals were different from one another?

5. What contrast existed for these two men beyond the grave? How did the rich man still regard Lazarus?

◆ **6.** What did the rich man call Abraham? What did Abraham call him in return?

♦ **7.** What does Abraham's answer to the rich man's request tell us about the reality of heaven and hell? What does the rich man's second request reveal about the finality of his situation?

8. What do you find significant about the exchange that followed in verses 29-31? What warning was Jesus giving here?

9. Why did the rich man end up in hell? Why did Lazarus go to Abraham's bosom? Is it wrong to be rich?

10. To whom did Jesus tell this parable about the rich man and Lazarus (see Luke 16:14)? Did news of his resurrection later cause these Jewish leaders to believe?

11. What do you think is the main point of this story? Why won't people believe even if someone returns from the dead?

12. How can the reality of hell affect your prayer life and your witness?

THE TEN MINAS

Luke 19:11-27; Matthew 25:14-30

Jesus told this parable while traveling to Jerusalem with his disciples. They were expecting him to display his power and set up his messianic kingdom there, but his real reason for going to the Holy City was to die. They needed to know that he would soon depart from this world in order to establish a heavenly kingdom rather than an earthly one. They also needed to know how he expected them to occupy themselves while he was gone, and how he would reward them for faithful service when he returned.

1. In what ways does your expectation of Jesus' return to earth influence the ways you invest your time now?

Read Luke 19:11-27.

◆ **2.** What does the story tell about the king? List all the facts you can find.

◆ **3.** What trust did the king place in his servants? What was his expectation?

4. When the king came home, what differences did he find in the returns his servants presented him? Why did two of the servants go right to work to enlarge their gifts, and how did he reward them?

5. What emotions do you feel as you consider the fate of the servant who hid the money? On what basis was he judged?

6. Who got the wicked servant's money? Who objected to this decision, and why? What was the king's reasoning?

7. Who do you think is represented by the king and the servants in this story?

8. Describe the kind of person illustrated by the servant who hid his gift. What are his good points and his weaknesses?

9. With which servant do you identify the most? Why?

♦ **10.** What principles underlie the king's test of his servants? The different rewards?

Read Matthew 25:14-30.

11. What similar principles do you find in this related parable?

12. Analyze the work you do for God. What keeps you at times from being a faithful servant?

Pray together that you will be wise stewards of the gifts God has given you.

THE GOOD SAMARITAN

Luke 10:25-37

A man in the crowd had a debate going on in his head as he listened to Jesus. He was the legal expert—a religious lawyer, a scribe—and his manner betrayed pride in his authority. Perhaps as he planned to question Jesus, he had mentally reviewed the scenario and had in mind the direction his arguments would take. Jesus answered the lawyer's question with perhaps the most familiar and best-loved of all the parables—the story of an innocent victim and a compassionate neighbor.

1. Think of someone who has been a good neighbor to you. What about the person's life has made you feel that way?

Read Luke 10:25-37.

2. What was the lawyer's motivation in questioning Jesus about eternal life? How did Jesus avoid being caught in the net the lawyer laid for him?

3. What apparently happened to the lawyer as he quoted verses of Scripture in answer to Jesus' question (verse 29)? How did the lawyer try to avoid the implications of his answer? Why do you think Jesus gives him a story-answer rather than a technical argument?

◆ **4.** As the story opens, what happened to the traveler and what was his condition?

5. Who first came upon the wounded man? What do we expect of him?

♦ **6.** Describe the behavior of the second man. How might he and the priest have rationalized their actions?

♦ **7.** Who is really the main character in this story? How would a Jewish lawyer be likely to react to the nationality of the hero of this story?

8. Think of adjectives to characterize the Samaritan's response to the wounded man. List the verbs describing his actions. How long did he care for the wounded man?

♦ **9.** How was the question Jesus asked in verse 36 different from the one the lawyer asked in verse 29? Define the word *neighbor*. Does Jesus use this word as a noun or a verb?

10. What point did Jesus make in this parable? What did he want the lawyer (and us) to understand about himself?

11. What keeps us from showing mercy to others? Why is showing mercy a characteristic of genuine faith?

12. The parable has a second meaning. In what ways is Jesus like the Good Samaritan? Share with the group your own experience of Jesus acting as your "neighbor."

THE TENANTS

Matthew 21:33-46

Sometimes once is not enough. Through the ages God has communicated his plan of redemption again and again through his prophets. But again and again his people have rejected his servants. This hardheartedness was still true of the Jewish leaders in Jesus' day. In this last week of Jesus' earthly life the chief priests and Pharisees, nervous about the power Jesus was gaining over the crowds, were watching him closely. In this pointed parable Jesus steps all over their religious toes by confronting them with the truth.

1. What evidence can you relate of God's repeated overtures in your life to show his care for you?

Read Matthew 21:33-46.

2. Who owned the vineyard? What kind of man was he?

3. How did the tenants regard this owner? What happened to the tenants (verses 41, 43)?

♦   **4.** Identify the owner, the vineyard, and the tenants.

5. Who were the servants who were seized and mistreated? Why did the owner finally send his son?

6. What can we learn here about the privileges and freedoms God allows his "tenants"? About human responsibility?

7. Discuss what this story reveals to us about God.

♦ **8.** What does Jesus' telling of this parable show us about how he viewed himself? In what ways was Jesus a threat to the Jewish religious leaders?

9. After concluding his story, Jesus quoted part of Psalm 118 to his listeners. What four observations did he make about the "stone" in verses 42 and 44? Who is the stone?

10. Describe how the chief priests and Pharisees reacted to the story. Why didn't understanding the parable cause them to repent?

11. In what ways are you often like the tenants in this story? What "vineyard" in your life have you taken over as your own (image, career, success, property, talent, etc.)?

12. Which is the stronger theme in this parable: God's love or God's justice? Give evidence for your answer. Have you found this balance true in your own life?

13. Close with sentence prayers of confession and praise to our God who loves us so much in spite of our self-centeredness.

THE SHREWD MANAGER

Luke 16:1-13

On first reading this parable is one of the most difficult to interpret of all the stories Jesus told. The hero of the story turns out to be a scoundrel, a dubious figure indeed to teach us anything about the kingdom of God. Elsewhere Jesus compared his heavenly Father to a hard-hearted judge, and himself to a thief in the night. Perhaps Jesus used these images to shock his hearers into listening more closely and pondering more carefully. Though the behavior of the main character is not to be our model, we can see an important theme in this parable. The shrewd manager plays a minor role in showing us a greater truth about using our resources rightly and wisely.

1. Explain the difference between serving money and making money serve.

Read Luke 16:1-13.

2. Of what did the rich man accuse his manager? On what basis?

3. What dilemma did the manager face? How did he plan for the future?

♦ **4.** Whose money did he manipulate (verses 5-7)? What did he do with his master's accounts?

♦ **5.** Why do you think the master commended the manager? Does acting shrewdly have good or bad connotations? Why?

6. How much thought and effort do you suppose it took for the manager to carry off his scheme? With how much intelligence and effort do you put your money to work for the kingdom of God?

◆ **7.** How does Jesus' comment in verses 8-9 shed light on the point of this story?

8. What are the "true riches" of verse 11? What larger principle of stewardship is seen here?

9. Why does God demand such exclusive loyalty to himself? Why can't we love both God and money?

10. What happens to someone whose whole life is centered on money and the gaining of wealth?

11. How do you view your own worldly wealth? What questions can you ask yourself in order to better evaluate your use of money?

12. How can you use your money, property, and possessions for eternal purposes?

THE WORKERS IN THE VINEYARD

Matthew 20:1-16

The economics of the kingdom of God are markedly different from those of the secular world. "Seniority does not necessarily mean honor," wrote William Barclay. It was hard for both the Jewish leaders and the disciples to understand that in God's kingdom, there is no favored nation or master race. Just prior to the telling of this story, Peter had reminded Jesus that he and the other disciples had left everything to follow him. He implied that this deserved some special kind of reward. Jesus told this story to remind the disciples (and the Jews who listened) that God administers his kingdom by his own rules.

1. Describe a time when you felt that your good work for God went unrecognized. How did you respond in that situation, and why?

Read Matthew 20:1-16.

◆ **2.** What was the landowner's concern in this story? How often did he go out and recruit workers?

3. What seemed unfair in the payment of the workers? Put yourself in their place—how would you react, and why?

4. How did the landowner justify his action? Were those hired first deprived of anything because of the owner's action?

5. Summarize in your own words what Jesus was teaching in this story.

6. Who is the landowner in the story, and what does the vineyard represent?

♦ **7.** Who might be represented by the people hired first? Those hired later? How might this story have affected the religious Jews at this time?

♦ **8.** On what basis is anyone accepted into the kingdom of heaven? Distinguish between *injustice* and *grace*.

9. What do you think Jesus is saying in verse 16? How does this reverse our typical human values?

10. What attitude did Jesus want to see in his followers regarding their own service to him?

♦ **11.** Think of other biblical examples or illustrations of the "last shall be first" principle.

♦ **12.** Would you identify yourself as one who entered the kingdom early, or one who came later? How does this fact affect your motives for serving God, and your attitudes toward rewards?

13. What does this parable teach us about God's compassion?

Reflect on the following poem, and then pray together, thanking God that he has called you to work in his vineyard.

> Alas, that I so lately knew thee,
> Thee, so worthy of the best;
> Nor had sooner turned to thee,
> Truest good and only rest!
> The more I love, I mourn the more
> That I did not love before!
> —Johannes Scheffler

THE UNMERCIFUL SERVANT

Matthew 18:21-35

This parable follows Jesus' instructions about handling problems in close relationships. The principle he taught was that we must do whatever is necessary to heal any breach between believers. In the context of such reconciliation, he promised: "Where two or three come together in my name, there am I with them." Jesus was saying that he cares about the way conflicts are solved, and that he is present and personally involved in such occasions. Perhaps motivated by this teaching, Peter poses a sticky question about forgiveness to the Lord—one which we all must deal with.

1. Recall a situation in which you have been provoked or repeatedly wronged by someone. How did you handle it?

Read Matthew 18:21-35.

◆ **2.** Do you think Peter thought he was being generous in the number of times he suggested to forgive? What did Jesus think of his suggestion?

◆ **3.** What was Jesus really emphasizing in his answer? Are we to forgive someone only seventy-seven times?

◆ **4.** Look again at the story Jesus tells. Was the king being fair in his initial plan so that some payment could be made on the debt?

5. The man's debt would today be worth millions of dollars. What motivated the king to cancel the servant's entire debt?

6. The fellow servant's debt, translated into today's currency, would be worth a few dollars. Compare the first servant's behavior toward his fellow servant with the king's behavior toward him.

7. How did the other servants, and finally the king, view the man's actions?

8. Who does the king represent in this story? What did Jesus illustrate by the enormous contrast in the size of the two debts?

9. How do others' "debts" to you compare with your debt before God? What do you owe God?

◆ **10.** Express Jesus' concluding statement in verse 35 in your own words. Discuss the implications of this uncompromising statement.

11. Is this primarily a story about a king (who changes his mind about forgiven debts) or about a man who didn't understand *grace?*

12. How does your experience of grace affect your ability to forgive others?

13. Is there someone you need to forgive? Is there someone you need to contact, asking for forgiveness?

Close in prayer, praising God for the way he forgives our sins, and asking for his grace to help you forgive others.

THE COST OF DISCIPLESHIP

Luke 14:25-35

The crowds were thronging around Jesus, traveling with him wherever he went. They had never met a teacher or a healer like him. Only in the ancient tales of Israel had they heard of such a miracle worker. Jesus was concerned about this crowd and wanted them to see their own enthusiasm and adulation in its true light. In this double parable Jesus discourages superficial followers with two hard-hitting illustrations.

1. Many people feel they have to "keep their options open" for the future. What does this mean, and how is this thinking incongruent with being a disciple of Jesus?

Read Luke 14:25-35.

2. What was Jesus' intent in making the startling statements of verses 26-27? How could one who told us to love our enemies suggest that we hate those who are closest to us?

♦ **3.** What does *hate* mean in this context? Why does following Jesus demand such drastic loyalty?

♦ **4.** What does it mean to carry our cross? What is the significance of a cross?

5. What considerations must be weighed by both the builder and the king? What consequences must be avoided?

6. What is involved in following Jesus? (Think in personal terms.) What costs are to be estimated? What are the consequences of *not* counting the cost?

7. What causes people who at one time gave evidence of following Jesus to fall away?

♦ **8.** List some common properties or uses of salt. How is a half-hearted Christian like unsalty salt?

♦ **9.** What can this illustration teach us about sharing the gospel honestly with others?

10. What distinction is there between following a crowd (or a congregation) who follows Jesus and being a real disciple?

11. What are the rewards of discipleship?

12. In what ways have you had to count the cost in following Jesus? What has carrying your cross meant for you?

LOST THINGS

Luke 15

There's nothing quite like the joy and relief we feel when we find a valuable or precious object that has been lost. Jesus picks up on this very human experience and draws for us a picture of God as a caring and diligent loving Father who does not give up on us.

1. Relate a "lost and found" story that you've experienced. What determined how hard and long you searched for the item?

Read Luke 15.

2. What prompted Jesus to tell these stories? How did his view of sinners differ from the view of the Pharisees and the teachers of the law?

3. What three metaphors (word pictures) are used to describe God?

4. Was it good business sense for the shepherd to leave ninety-nine sheep and look for one stray? What motivated the shepherd's search?

♦ **5.** Where was the silver coin lost? Why did the woman search so diligently?

6. What does it mean for a person to be "lost"? According to the first two stories, what happens in heaven when lost ones are found?

♦ **7.** Skim verses 11-32 again. What reasons might the son have had for wanting his inheritance? Why do you think he would exchange his privileges as a son for independence? In what ways have men and women done the same today?

8. When did it occur to the son that he had lost his freedom? What does his rehearsed speech reveal?

9. Describe the father's response to the son. On what basis did the father receive him?

10. Why didn't the older brother join the festivities? How could the older brother live with his father and yet know so little of his heart?

11. Compare the three parables in this chapter. What are the differences? What are the similarities?

12. What do these stories tell you about God? What do you learn about yourself from these stories?

13. If there are parties in heaven for lost people who are found, and if the Father gives such a lavish welcome to his lost children, what emotional response do you have to God's welcoming you home?

Closing Thoughts

As you conclude this series, what new insights do you have concerning the use of story to communicate truth?

Name ways God has become more real to you through these stories.

LEADER'S NOTES

■ Study 1/The Sower and the Soils

Question 4. Did Jesus really mean here that he spoke in parables so that people would *not* understand? R.V.G. Tasker states that perhaps Jesus was withholding further truth about himself from the crowds because they had already proved to be deaf to his claims and unresponsive to him (R.V.G. Tasker, "The Gospel According to Matthew," *Tyndale New Testament Commentary,* p. 134. London: The Tyndale Press, 1961). See Matthew 13:14-15, where Jesus implies that their deafness and blindness was deliberate. It may well be that his parables test spiritual responsiveness, and that only those who are open to hear really do hear.

Question 8. Matthew 19:16-22 gives us an example of someone like thorny soil. The man's wealth was not bad in itself, but it was in the way of his truly following Jesus.

■ Study 2/The Two Weddings

Question 2. According to ancient Jewish social custom, when invitations to a great feast were sent out, the specific time was not stated.

When everything was ready, servants were sent with a final summons to the guests to come.

Question 4. Clothing and garments are sometimes used in Scripture as a picture of our salvation and new life in Christ (see Isaiah 61:10 and Romans 13:14).

Question 8. In the Middle East a wedding meant a week-long celebration. The climax of the week was the bridegroom's arrival to claim his bride, who was waiting for him with her bridesmaids. With their oil lamps the bridesmaids then lighted the way for the wedding procession. But the actual time of the bridegroom's arrival was a secret, a surprise. The bride and her attendants had to be ready for the messenger sent ahead to announce the groom's arrival.

▧ Study 3/The Kingdom of Heaven

Question 3. These weeds are *darnel,* a somewhat poisonous weed, which at first looks like wheat, and cannot be distinguished from it until harvest time, when the mature seed-heads look obviously different from wheat. Farmers often threatened to sow such weeds in an enemy's field. It was such a common practice that the Romans made it illegal.

Question 7. "The dangerous people in the church are those who celebrate Christmas, Good Friday, Easter, and Pentecost without realizing and experiencing for themselves the death, resurrection, and indwelling power of Christ. It is possible to hear the good news of God's love in Christ without letting him love us personally in the depth of our need. It seems ridiculous and incredulous, but thousands attend church and call themselves Christians but never know the joy of abiding in Christ and allowing him to abide in them. They look and act like wheat, but are tares" (Lloyd Ogilvie, *Autobiography of God*, p. 84. Glendale, Calif.: Regal Books, 1979).

Study 4/The Rich Man and Lazarus

Question 2. In the Greek, the last phrase of Luke 16:19 conveys the sense of feeding consistently on exotic and costly foods. The rich man is traditionally referred to as *Dives* in other literature. *Dives* is Latin for "rich."

Question 3. Lazarus is the only character in all of Jesus' parables who had a name. *Lazarus* means "God is my help."

Question 6. Use of "father" and "son" is a clue that Jesus was speaking to orthodox Jews who were "rich" in tradition and rule-keeping, and were technically "sons of Abraham."

Question 7. "Here in the extremity of his need the rich man feels, for the first time, something like love. Of all places, he feels it in hell, where at best he may feel it but no longer exercise it, where it lies dammed up within him, incapable of expression and causing him only torment" (Helmut Thielicke, *The Waiting Father,* p. 49. New York: Harper & Row, 1959).

Study 5/The Ten Minas

Question 2. Palestine was part of the Roman Empire at this time, and various members of the ruling family would travel to Rome to be confirmed in their power to rule over their particular area. When Herod the Great died, he left the kingdom divided, and the Jews sent an embassy of fifty men to Rome to object to Herod's son, Archelaus, being made their king. Jesus often used contemporary events to illustrate truth in his parables. Anyone in Judea would recognize this historical incident in the words of Luke 19:14.

Question 3. A *mina* was about three months' wages.

Question 10. God has given us gifts and resources to use for the benefit of the kingdom. He "expects us to use these talents so that they multiply and the kingdom grows. He asks each of us to account for what we do with his gifts. While awaiting the coming of the kingdom of God in glory, we must do Christ's work" *(Life Application Bible,* p. 1846. Wheaton, Ill.: Tyndale House, 1988).

◼ Study 6/The Good Samaritan

Question 4. Everyone listening to the parable could picture the scene. The road from Jerusalem to Jericho descends 3600 feet. Robbers were often concealed among the rocks along this twenty-two-mile winding road with hidden turns. It was commonly called the "Bloody Way."

Question 6. "The priest and Levite may have feared defilement by touching a corpse" *(The New Bible Commentary: Revised,* p. 905. Grand Rapids, Mich.: Eerdmans, 1970). See Numbers 19:11-13.

Question 7. The Jews would have nothing to do with Samaritans. In 722 B.C. most of the Jewish population of Samaria was exiled to Babylon. Those who remained behind eventually intermarried with the Assyrians who conquered the land. The descendants, the Samaritans, were thus considered half-breeds.

Question 9. "The lawyer had 'lost face' by being given this textbook answer, and tried to regain the initiative by demanding a more precise definition of his neighbour. The parable given in reply is most remarkable. . . . For although the lawyer asked '*Who* is my neighbour (passively understood)?' Jesus suggests that the real question is rather 'Do *I* behave as a neighbour (active sense)?' In other words, Jesus does not supply information as to whom one should help, for failure to keep the commandment does not spring from lack of information but from lack of love. It was not fresh knowledge that the lawyer needed, but a new heart" *(New Bible Commentary: Revised,* p. 905).

Study 7/The Tenants

Question 4. "The main elements in this parable are (1) the land-owner—God, (2) the vineyard—Israel, (3) the tenants—the Jewish religious leaders, (4) the landowner's servants—the prophets and priests who remained faithful to God and preached to Israel, (5) the son—Jesus (Matthew 21:38), and (6) the other tenants—the Gentiles" *(Life Application Bible,* p. 1697).

Question 8. "The leaders of Israel wanted no one to threaten their authority over the vineyard they controlled. Not even a rabbi from Nazareth. When he rode into their Jerusalem, it was the landowner's son approaching the vineyard" *(Autobiography of God,* p. 275).

Study 8/The Shrewd Manager

Question 4. "A steward, entrusted with his master's estate and accounts, was suspected of mismanaging his affairs, if not of actually behaving dishonestly. When he realized that he was in danger of dismissal, he summoned his master's debtors and allowed each one to enter a lower figure on his IOU or promissory note. The debtors would thus feel indebted to the steward and help him when he was out of a job. He had acted with commendable astuteness in providing for his own interests" *(The New Bible Commentary: Revised,* p. 912).

Question 5. "Jesus is not commending his theft—the man is described as 'dishonest.' But he illustrates the believer's need for astuteness, initiative, and ingenuity. The dishonest steward was wise enough to make his present opportunities serve his future welfare" (Gladys Hunt, *Luke: A Daily Dialogue With God,* p. 119. Wheaton, Ill.: Shaw Publishers, 1986).

Question 7. There are various interpretations of the main point of this parable. "a. The parable may simply urge men to prepare for the crisis brought about by the ministry of Jesus with the same zeal of the steward facing an uncertain future. b. Jesus commented that astuteness is shown much more by worldly people than by those who belong to the new era. Men should learn from the steward and use their wealth to make God their friend, so that, when money is no longer of any help to them, God may receive them into his presence. . . c. Keeping the law and showing generosity are the ways for wealthy people to gain God's approval. None of these interpretations can be excluded" *(The New Bible Commentary: Revised,* pp. 912-13). "The Lord implied that earthly property can be used to help others, whose gratitude will ensure a welcome in eternity" *(Wycliffe Bible Commentary,* p. 1055. Chicago: Moody Press, 1973).

■ Study 9/The Workers in the Vineyard

Question 2. The third hour was 9 A.M. The sixth, ninth, and eleventh hours were noon, 3 P.M., and 5 P.M. respectively.

Question 7. "Jesus further clarifies the membership rules of the kingdom of heaven—entrance is by God's grace alone. In this parable, God is the landowner, and believers are the workers. This parable speaks especially to those who feel superior because of heritage or favored position, to those who feel superior because they have spent so much time with Christ, and to new believers as reassurance of God's grace" *(Life Application Bible,* p. 1693).

Question 8. "We did not choose Christ: He chose us long before our desire to respond to his love. He was at work in us creating in us the longing for him to fill our emptiness. So there is absolutely no credit to us that we are at work in the Lord's vineyard. We are there, early or later, by sheer grace" *(Autobiography of God,* p. 270).

Question 11. Allow some thinking time for this question. Luke 23:39-43 is one example.

Question 12. Fellowship with and service for Jesus are not business transactions; the rewards are on a different level entirely. No one who meets Jesus and enters the kingdom late will be proud of squandered time, and those who meet him early and grow slowly into deep fellowship with him will still long to have known him sooner.

Study 10/The Unmerciful Servant

Question 2. Rabbinic teaching was that a man should forgive his brother—but only three times. Rabbi Jose ben Hanina taught: "He who begs forgiveness from his neighbor must not do so more than three times."

Question 3. Some versions read "seventy-seven times"; others say "seventy times seven."

Question 4. "In Bible times, serious consequences awaited those who could not pay their debts. A person lending money could seize the borrower who couldn't pay and force him or his family to work until the debt was paid. The debtor could also be thrown into prison, or his family could be sold into slavery to help pay off the debt. It was hoped that the debtor, while in prison, would sell off his landholdings or that relatives would pay the debt. If not, the debtor could remain in prison for life" *(Life Application Bible, p. 1690).*

Question 10. "Not all the details of the parable are to be pressed. But the point is clear that the unforgiving man cannot be in a position of forgiveness before God. The man forgiven by God through what Christ has done will give in his treatment of others unmistakable evidence of his gratitude to and dependence upon [God]" *(The New Bible Commentary: Revised, p. 840).*

■ Study 11/The Cost of Discipleship

Question 3. "Hate means 'love less' (see Matthew 10:37)" *(The New Bible Commentary: Revised, p. 911).*

Question 4. "Jesus' audience was well aware of what it meant to carry one's own cross. When the Romans led a criminal to his execution site, he was forced to carry the cross on which he would die. This showed his submission to Rome and warned observers that they had better submit too. Jesus spoke this teaching to get the crowds to think through their enthusiasm for him. He encouraged those who were superficial either to go deeper or to turn back" *(Life Application Bible, p. 1836).*

Question 8. The salt generally used for seasoning and preserving food was from the soil around the Dead Sea. It was impure, mixed with gravel and other minerals, and rain would often dissolve the salt away, leaving a saltless residue—a salt that had lost its saltiness.

Question 9. Jesus would not recruit disciples under false pretenses. Neither should we. The Christian life involves getting off the throne of your own life, and letting Jesus reign there.

■ Study 12/Lost Things

Question 5. The coin was probably a drachma, worth a day's wages in Jesus' time, about twenty cents in our currency. Such a coin would, however, have sentimental as well as monetary value, probably being one of the ten coins sewn to a headband and given to a Jewish woman by her husband as a wedding gift. To lose it would be like losing a gem from one's wedding ring.

Question 7. "The younger son's share of the estate would have been one-third, with the older son receiving two-thirds. In most cases he would have received this at his father's death, although fathers sometimes chose to divide up their inheritance early and retire from managing their estates. What is unusual here is that the younger one initiated the division of the estate. This showed arrogant disregard for his father's authority as head of the family" *(Life Application Bible,* p. 1837).

WHAT SHOULD WE STUDY NEXT?

To help your group answer that question, we've listed the Fisherman Guides by category so you can choose your next study.

TOPICAL STUDIES

Becoming Women of Purpose, Barton

Building Your House on the Lord, Brestin

Discipleship, Reapsome

Doing Justice, Showing Mercy, Wright

Encouraging Others, Johnson

Examining the Claims of Jesus, Brestin

Friendship, Brestin

The Fruit of the Spirit, Briscoe

Great Doctrines of the Bible, Board

Great Passages of the Bible, Plueddemann

Great People of the Bible, Plueddemann

Great Prayers of the Bible, Plueddemann

Growing Through Life's Challenges, Reapsome

Guidance & God's Will, Stark

Higher Ground, Brestin

How Should a Christian Live? (1,2, & 3 John), Brestin

Marriage, Stevens

Moneywise, Larsen

One Body, One Spirit, Larsen

The Parables of Jesus, Hunt

Prayer, Jones

The Prophets, Wright

Proverbs & Parables, Brestin

Relationships, Hunt

Satisfying Work, Stevens & Schoberg

Senior Saints, Reapsome

Sermon on the Mount, Hunt

The Ten Commandments, Briscoe

When Servants Suffer, Rhodes

Who Is Jesus? Van Reken

Worship, Sibley

BIBLE BOOK STUDIES

Genesis, Fromer & Keyes

Job, Klug

Psalms, Klug

Proverbs: Wisdom That Works, Wright

Ecclesiastes, Brestin

Jonah, Habakkuk, & Malachi, Fromer & Keyes

Matthew, Sibley

Mark, Christensen

Luke, Keyes

John: Living Word, Kuniholm

Acts 1-12, Christensen

Paul (Acts 13-28), Christensen

Romans: The Christian Story, Reapsome

1 Corinthians, Hummel

Strengthened to Serve (2 Corinthians), Plueddemann

Galatians, Titus & Philemon, Kuniholm

Ephesians, Baylis

Philippians, Klug

Colossians, Shaw

Letters to the Thessalonians, Fromer & Keyes

Letters to Timothy, Fromer & Keyes

Hebrews, Hunt

James, Christensen

1 & 2 Peter, Jude, Brestin

How Should a Christian Live? (1, 2 & 3 John), Brestin

Revelation, Hunt

BIBLE CHARACTER STUDIES

Ruth & Daniel, Stokes

David: Man after God's Own Heart, Castleman

Job, Klug

King David: Trusting God for a Lifetime, Castleman

Elijah, Castleman

Men Like Us, Heidebrecht & Scheuermann

Peter, Castleman

Paul (Acts 13-28), Christensen

Great People of the Bible, Plueddemann

Women Like Us, Barton

Women Who Achieved for God, Christensen

Women Who Believed God, Christensen